FREE

ISBN 978-1-7933-1971-5

Printed in the United States of America

Acknowledgments

Special thank you to my family and friends who have been there for me even when they did not know the depth of my pain. To my parents Freddie and Bessie Brinson, my brother Gerard, my sisters Valorie and Alicia, and my children who have seen the good, the bad, the joy and the peace that we have now; I love you. To my former Pastor Sherlene McClary of Greater Deliverance Church, my spiritual home when I could not go home. Thank you Pastor McClary for always being there, day or night, and for allowing me to work with Youth in Action and in ministry. To the ladies of Greater Deliverance, Gloria, Renee, and Othaey, who shared their homes, food, and gave me a sense of safety when I had nowhere else to go. I love you all! Without your support, I would not have been able to leave and have the courage to start over again.

To my current Pastors John and Constance Poitier-Christian of Christian Worship Center, I love you all for loving me, even when I did not believe in myself, and for always supporting. Thank you to my Christian Worship Center family for allowing me to work in ministry and share my gifts and talents while God helped me to heal: mind, body, and soul. For being there for Makai, Marsellus, and Murcer Simmons and never letting distance keep you from always covering our family.

To my college roommate, my sister from another mother, Nicole Clark Allen. College was the best of times and the worst of times for me, but thank you for always listening, being a real friend, and never changing. I believe in you and you believe in me; the best is yet to come for us. We have a special bond that will never be broken. Love you my sister!

Special thank you to the Victory Over Violence team who helped take my God-given vision of a non-profit to support survivors to walk in Victory and made it happen; my team V.P. Nicole Allen and Treasurer/Secretary Bessie Brinson. My creative artist and décor consultants Kenesha Haugabrook and Tiffany Myles Poitier. My Uncle Jerry and Aunt Wanda Morell, your love for life and each other inspired me throughout this journey, and I thank God for your union. To my special consultant, Cherrise Wilks, such a strong young woman and positive voice; thank you for believing in my vision. My forever friend and web designer, Dante' Harmon, I am eternally grateful for you always listening, offering advice, and never judging; thank you for being there and encouraging me to make this step. Because of each of you, I am free and walking in victory one day at a time.

Thank you Dr. Vernetta Williams for helping me give my words life!

Foreword

Often, in passing, we overlook someone because we see them, but we don't quite see into them. Lorrie's redemptive and compelling story "Free" is a must read for men and women alike, especially those who have grown up in organized religion. This book is life changing, and I am extremely proud of Lorrie for being transparent.

Dantè Harmon

Friend & CEO of Dagape Music

Preface

FREE is a book about the early years of my life. It was written not only to give some life lessons, but also to share my truth about my encounters with sexual assault, aka date rape, and domestic violence. Abuse, whether physically, emotionally, or financially, is never okay. I want each survivor or family member of these victims to realize that love doesn't hurt; each survivor can begin again and experience a life of hope and happiness after the pain. You are not what happened to you. You are who God says you are, and freedom is accessible to each person. In describing my early years, this book shares the keys to freedom and living a life in victory and overcoming the hurts of the past.

Dedication

This book is dedicated to the victims of sexual assault and domestic violence, to all survivors, like me, who remained silent and allowed the stigma and shame of being sexually violated to keep them from sharing their truth. This book is also dedicated to survivors of domestic battery and domestic assault; those who felt that they could not break free and start over again. Finally, I dedicate this book to my mother, the strongest woman I know, my sisters, and my nieces. We will break this generational curse and walk in victory one day at a time.

I AM

I am not the little girl who grew up with no father. No, I had a home with a father and mother. I am not the lies that people said about me because they were jealous of me or didn't understand me. I am not what happened to me because the enemy was working even then to kill me. I am not the pain I felt from the inside out or the pain I suffered while trying to get out. But I am what I am today because God used my pain and gave me purpose. I am no longer afraid; I am courageous

I am no longer bound; I am free

I am no longer a victim; I am victorious

I am not what happened to me;

I am beautifully and wonderfully made.

Table of Contents

A Sense of Freedom

I grew up in a small city in Central Florida of less than 50,000 residents and only 1 high school, but I didn't see limits on what I could do. Learning new things learning a new sport, or making a new friend was not a challenge for me.

My parents were hard workers who devoted themselves to church and serving people. Church was their life, and they taught us, at an early age, that church, work, and school were the most important aspects of life. We attended church twice on Sunday, then Wednesday and Friday nights. Between choir rehearsals, youth, conventions, assemblies, and district meetings, it seemed we were always in church. I always saw my dad go to work. My mom always worked hard, cooked daily, and cleaned; she was a seamstress and baker. I had two older sisters; Valorie was 10 years older and Alicia 18 months older. My older brother,

Freddie Jr. who passed away before seeing his 50th birthday. I was the baby girl, daddy's girl, who usually got what I wanted if it was in my dad's power to get it. But then came my younger brother, Gerard who is 10 years younger than me, but I remained baby girl.

I knew I wanted to be an accountant since middle school, when I worked in my dad's office at the Appliance Repair business, recording sales and service calls and writing up deposits. I didn't want kids or to get married. I simply wanted to be an accountant, have my own place, and travel. From softball to cheerleading to the National Junior Honor Society, my desire to succeed and be the best I could be was my mission. I wanted to make my parents proud and they always encouraged us to do our best.

High School became more of a challenge than middle school. The dynamics changed in high school because I had my older sister, cousins, and people on campus who could care less who I was. My friends in honors classes and my fellow cheerleaders were all who really mattered, or at least that's what I thought. Being the only black cheerleader, the only black girl in my honors and gifted classes proved to be difficult and uncomfortable at times. Not feeling accepted by my own black classmates and sometimes teased for being in honors or gifted classes made me unhappy and sometimes angry because it just did not feel fair. So I dealt with the idea of not being accepted the best I knew how at such an early age, I joined clubs, band, I was cheerleader, ran track, and anything else that would put me in a space where I felt accepted and a part of something with other students like me.

My small church growing up was Pentecostal, but a part of a larger denomination of churches called The House of God Church. My Aunt was the Pastor and most of my family attended the same church. In between church services were choir rehearsals, youth gatherings, and any meetings my parents may have had. My dad was the Chairman Deacon and mom, by the time I got to high school, was also a Pastor at a mission church in Crystal River, which meant when the church doors opened, we had to go. My siblings and I were not always that excited about going to church all the time. I would get an attitude every time I missed an event at school because of church. Especially when we had services on Friday nights when basketball or football season had started. My parents asked no questions; You get your skirt on and you get in the van and head off to church.

By the time I was halfway through high school, I had my sights set on getting away from Leesburg. My desire was to go to Tallahassee to attend Florida State University; less than 4 hours from home, but it was out of Leesburg. I knew if I kept my grades up, then scholarships were my ticket out of Leesburg. When it came to boyfriends, well, that was just a no, according to my parents. More like an absolutely not! Nonetheless, my sister and I had boyfriends. Unlike my sister, Alicia, who was a phenomenal athlete, kind hearted person, and just a year ahead of me, I didn't maintain relationships well with guys in school. Alicia had the same boyfriend from middle school to high school. I had a boyfriend in middle school but dumped him to pick up another one before high school. I wouldn't call it dating because we weren't allowed to date until around the age of 16, which still meant nothing because we weren't allowed to go anywhere with our boyfriends, not even to the movies. The only dances we could attend were Homecoming and Prom. Most boys in our little town didn't want to deal with "the Brinson girls" because they already knew our parents were strict. You could come to the fence of our home and visit, but those boys better be gone, before the parents pulled up to the yard. As preachers' kids, we found a way to see our boyfriends, with or without permission, it seemed unfair that dating was not a topic of discussion at the time, so finding a way to do what seemed like all teenagers were doing which was spending time with friends and dating required a little creativity and some stretching of the truth at times.

But I figured out quickly that I didn't want to be tied down to one guy; it was like being married, which I had decided already that I didn't want to be married. My junior year in high school, caught up in my emotions and feelings after a school dance, I lost my virginity to my boyfriend, it was not pretty, it was not a happy moment, I was scared, and I don't think either of us really knew what we were doing. But we were in "love" and wanted to experience what I thought would be some amazing moment, but it hurt, and I cried myself to sleep that night and never told anyone. Within a year we broke up. The break up was not mutual, he was angry, but I felt like he was trying to control me. He wanted to tell me what I could wear and couldn't wear and where I was going to be and when; he seemed so jealous. That first break up was difficult because I had not experienced those type of emotions with any guy, and I was so young. I regretted the secrets I had to hide and lies I had to tell just to see him and be with him. Most of all, I regretted that I would be graduating soon and was no longer a virgin. He had become so possessive, and I couldn't handle it at that age. I just wanted to move on with getting out of high school. My sights were set on graduating soon with multiple scholarships, applying to Florida State University (FSU), and leaving home in another year. I was ready for a new start and atmosphere, so I decided to focus on doing my best to make sure it would happen. At that point, I had a boyfriend, but he was not a priority and was not at my high school and dealing with some overly possessive guy that I had to run into everyday was not on my list. I only dreamed of having fun my senior year and anxiously awaiting my acceptance letter from FSU. The letter arrived in December; I remember walking to the mailbox at the corner down from our house. I didn't open the envelope till I got home, I remember it being a thick envelope with the housing information and orientation information. My prayers were answered, I was accepted to The Florida State University, a place I had dreamt about since learning about the school when I was 6 years old. I was so excited, I will never forget it because it was one of the best days of my life. I felt like all my hard work in academics in high school and the sacrifices and commitment to myself I made paid off. By May, I had multiple scholarships and grants. My tuition, books, and housing were fully paid. I was ready for my new start in my new dormitory at Florida State.

I remember arriving on campus the week before college started with all the other freshman for orientation. Getting out of my parents' van and walking on campus that August morning. The air was warm, and I remember thinking, "It's finally here; I have finally arrived!" As we began walking up one of several hills to our first meeting for freshman orientation, I was so excited, but my parents were not as excited. They were happy for me, I was the first of their children to leave home for college. But my parents were also worried that in less than 48 hours, they would be leaving me, their baby girl in Tallahassee without them. My older sisters Valorie and Alicia attended school at the local community college at the time. But I would be the first to leave Leesburg and my family was happy for me and supported my decision to go to FSU which made the idea of moving away from home as a Freshman in college better for me.

I met several students immediately at orientation;

little did I know that these four, 2 guys and 2 girls from South Florida, would eventually become lifelong friends. The five of us including me immediately bonded that week. After listening to the counselors about the "Do's and Don'ts" of campus life, we all agreed that we wouldn't leave each other anywhere. Drinking and partying and living out of control, that went along with the college life was something that each of us took seriously. Date rape, college women getting snatched and assaulted around campus was prevalent and not just a myth. We agreed we would never walk alone, we would never attend a party alone, and we would always be in parties of two or more, always looking out for each other as sisters and brothers. There were my 2 new brothers from Dade County and my new sister from Palm Beach County and my new roommate from Dade County all different, but street smart, intelligent classmates, but I knew these four friends would be my new family and I had chosen the right place for my college career.

I thought dorm life would be easy, but I chose a co-ed

dorm, which I learned quickly came with its own set of problems. Kellum Hall had boys on 1 floor and alternated with girls on every other floor. I was in the Leadership Genesis Programs, on the 8th floor of the dorm, which meant boys were on the floor on the south side of the elevators and girls were on the north side of the elevators. Late night false alarms, panty raids, lights out in the hallways, and broken elevators was not exactly what I had imagined for my freshman year and a healthy learning experience. But I survived with the help of my new family at college and friends. We stayed together, we partied together, we studied together, we even attended church together, and I learned to survive!

Near the end of our first year, one of my sisters from Palm Beach, Nicole, who eventually became my best friend, and I decided to explore moving off campus into our own place. We felt like we matured, survived our freshman year with no major incidents and learned to watch out for each other and take care of one another. So, the search began for a

2 bedroom/2 bath apartment. It would be perfect to have a place where our friends could hang out with no curfews or dorm rules. We found the perfect 2/2 apartment less than 5 miles from campus and decided to move in the summer. Our brothers remained on campus and our other sister, also moved off campus into an apartment. Even though we moved away, we would still see each other on campus and maintain that relationship. Nicole and I each had our own bedroom, bathroom, and vehicle to drive. We would start our sophomore year off campus in our own place; it was an exciting time!

The Loss of Freedom

Once the fall semester started, my friend and I quickly missed some of the advantages of being on campus, like parking, campus events, and getting to class easily. Another issue that came up rather quickly was visitation by the opposite sex. In the dorms, visitation was limited to certain hours. In my co-ed dorm, visits were a little more liberal, but the guy still had to be out of the room by a certain time.

My experience with men and being alone with a man whenever I wanted was somewhat limited until my freshman year of college. I had a couple of boyfriends during my senior year of high school, but my learning curve on dating took a steep curve my first year of college. Being the daughter of a preacher, aka a "pk," came with many restrictions growing up. Certain topics were not discussed, like boyfriends, dating, and sex; no one said we couldn't discuss them, we just didn't. Having a boyfriend in college was hard. Hard because anyone I was seeing back home assumed, I was seeing someone at school. So real relationships I learned quickly were just too hard. My limited experience and knowledge of the world were exposed during my freshman year, but with the help of my new college friends and my family in Tallahassee, I had to learn the mind games that could be played on naïve young women like me. College men would prey on freshman girls. It was easy for a man to have a girlfriend at FSU, FAMU, TCC, and his high school sweetheart back home. The lessons I learned living on campus and dorm life were elementary compared to what I was about to experience on my own, off campus.

Many of my dorm friends and acquaintances got caught up in alcohol, drugs, sex, and partying when they left home. For students like me, who grew up in a strict household where those things were off limits, the curiosity of those activities forever linger in our minds. But, what's often not talked about are the sexual deviance and perversion that so commonly occurs on and off campus. It often follows this plot: boy meets girl, girl lets the boy talk her into going to his place, only for the girl to have sex and be recorded unknowingly. My roommate, Nicole and I decided to keep our pact and not go alone to any parties; we also agreed to only bring friends over if we both were home. Nicole was 19, and I was 18 years old and we felt we ready and safe in our place in our space.

After a couple of months in the off-campus apartment, I felt that I was on to whatever games would be played and could handle myself as a woman. My roommate had a pretty good guy. Although I was seeing someone on and off, but nothing ever serious because I really was not up for games and empty promises anymore. He was my friend and I understood our arrangement, whether that be intimacy or just friendship, I felt safe with him, and I settled for that because I knew him, and he knew me. Although brief, some of my past relationships with guys were too emotional for me being so young, so I would simply break up and move on. I felt that I had gotten past the self-esteem issues I continued to battle from high school about my weight and size. But I was always hard on myself about my weight, size, and not being quite good enough even in middle school. For a long time, I was the only "black cheerleader" and guys in high school found me attractive. I got attention that way. They would tell me about my beautiful legs, yet I thought, "But, they're too big." They would tell me how thick I was, yet I would say, "But, I'm fat." The attention, especially from the persistent bad boy and athlete, always got me. My parents did not like the guys I was attracted to and forbid it, but I was not in Leesburg anymore. I stopped playing that complex and view of myself in my head and simply wanted to be in a real relationship or have someone I could start something special with. When guys complimented me, I had the hardest time accepting it. As a sophomore in her own apartment, I could make my own decisions. But, relationships had not gone well for me since moving to Tallahassee. I had been lied to multiple times, dumped twice, proposed to once, and had cheated, so my track record was getting a little sketchy and pathetic. Yet, I thought that I was ready.

It was the fall semester, which was football season in Tallahassee. There was always plenty of my type of guys to choose from during that time of year. I met a guy; I vaguely remember where and which mall I met him at in Tallahassee. I do remember that he was a basketball player from another university; he was a big, tall, handsome guy. He was like a 280-pound teddy bear. I must say that I was somewhat attracted to him. He was so kind from day one. He asked me out after a few conversations, and I was so excited to be going on a real date. College men seldom had money for a real date, so many times, we would just "hang out" or meet up at the movies or the club or get a phone call at 11:45 pm for sex. I was excited to have a date.

I remember it was a little chilly in the air that night as it often is in late fall in Tallahassee. I had given him my apartment address; he picked me up in his truck and we went to dinner at a Chinese Restaurant on Tennessee Street one of the main roads that runs right down along Florida State campus. It was so nice to have a conversation and not sit and

25

wonder who would pay. We talked about him playing basketball at Ball State; he shared that he had friends on the FSU team that he was spending time with before going back to Miami then back to school. That night would be his last night in town, which made me a little sad because I wanted to get to know him better. But, I felt we must have had some connection because he was with me instead of hanging with the guys. I thought, "Wow, maybe he really does like me." I was all smiles as I thought, "I am special."

After leaving the restaurant, I remember him asking to come into the apartment before he left, and I agreed. It was all good because I figured my roommate was home, so no big deal. We got inside my apartment, and I didn't know if she was asleep, had company, or not back home yet, but I had let him in already. I was not prepared for what happened next. He went from a sweet teddy bear that I could squeeze to someone I never want to remember. He followed me down the hall, putting his almost 300 pounds on top of me on my bed and began saying in my face, "Tell me, you know you want some, come on, come on" as I tried to roll him off me as I told him to stop. I remember saying, "Stop Dre stop! What are you doing? Stop!" But, he just kept saying, "You know you want some; why you teasing me?" As he pulled up my dress and pushed himself inside me, I could smell his skin and feel his sweaty skin on me. I was being raped on my bed in my apartment. I remember him dripping sweat and his breath blowing in my face as he kept going as if he didn't hear me say, "Stop, get off me!"

I was not able to get from under what was once a teddy bear who had turned into an evil monster raping me in my bed. Finally, he stopped and immediately got up, closed his pants and said to me, "I don't know why you was trippin' you know you wanted it" and walked out. I don't remember what I said, but I remember being shocked and freaking out. A million questions started running through my head, *what just happened? Did he just take it? Did he even have on a rubber? Did he just rape me? What just happened? He set me up! Oh my God, oh my God?* I cried. I was in a rage. *He's* gone. *He just raped me!*

A thousand questions and thoughts kept running through my head. *What am I going to do? Where is my roommate? Should I call the cops? What am I going to say? Why was he here? Maybe I shouldn't have let him in? He wasn't supposed to be here. I let him in. I shouldn't have let him in. I shouldn't have worn a dress. Did I lead him on? Didn't he hear me say stop? What if I am pregnant?* The questions kept ringing through my head while I began having a dialogue with myself, *I thought he really liked me. I feel so stupid, just dumb, why was I so naïve in thinking he was really interested in me?* Crying in shame and disgusted with myself, I didn't even remember his last name….

I felt that night was the beginning of the end for me. Disgusted with my choice, I decided not to tell my family. I kept the painful, humiliating secret to myself. No one knew my pain, I was ashamed. Unfortunately, being raped was only the beginning of tragic events for me that school year. Shortly after being assaulted, my apartment was flooded during one of the many rainstorms in Tallahassee. Suddenly, my roommate and I were homeless and had to find another apartment. Staying in a hotel then my relative's couch was more stressful.

Making matters worse, I began having health issues because of the rape and made an appointment to see my gynecologist, only to learn the disgusting animal gave me a disease. It was a condition that eventually would lead to precancerous cells on my cervix and possibly infertility. The doctors were able to treat me. But, all the physical pain and disruption were because of contact with this monster who raped me, which resulted in a disease that would end my chances of being with another man or having children. Once the doctor found precancerous cells on my cervix, which would have developed into something much worse, laser surgery was required to remove the dangerous cells.

The surgery was necessary to save my chances of having a normal sex life and children, if I wanted them one day. The anger rose back up in me when the doctor delivered the news. Thoughts and questions bombarded my mind once again: *Surgery in the middle of the semester? How would I pay for that? What do I tell my family? Who will be there for me after surgery? I can't ask my roommate to take care of me; she has classes; it's midterms.*

I felt so alone, and it hurt. I was alone with my never-ending thoughts: *Flirting with promiscuity my freshman year led me to be a victim of rape my sophomore year; maybe it was my punishment for the choices I had made. Choices I knew were wrong, yet I did it, and it had caught up to me.* I wanted a change. I wanted to be free from the guilt that was becoming depressing. The secret and disappointment had become a distraction from studying and trying to do my best in school. I knew it was time to make better decisions and get my life back on track.

Freedom Reborn

After the surgery, life was hard. The first few days after surgery my sister, Alicia was with me during recovery. Even though we had begun bonding since leaving home from college, I still did not share with her what happened to me. It was still too painful and hard. Being angry at myself caused me to have a bad attitude about everything; it was a lonely place to not accept and love myself. Not loving myself made it hard to accept that someone else could love me. Still questioning my decisions and why I couldn't get pass the assault and what happened that night. Mentally and emotionally drained trying to focus on finishing the semester after getting behind during recovery after surgery was stressful. Not wanting to share with anyone and not being truthful about what happened to me and why I had to have surgery I was struggling just to go to class and focus. I couldn't go home and let my family see me falling apart emotionally. Summer of 1994 going into my Junior year, I knew something had to change. I knew that I could be better and do better and something in me would not let me just give up and go home. God allowed me to make it through a very tough academic year despite what I dealt with mentally, emotionally, physically, I was grateful. Not just because he kept me, but I passed all my classes and my exams. I knew it was only God, I didn't feel like I deserved it, but I was so grateful, my heart was full. I felt like I owed God more; I began attending church more regularly, attending bible study weekly, and meeting other young college students at Watson Temple. I never forgot what my parents taught me growing up in church about the power of prayer and gathering together even though I didn't go to church like I did growing up. The foundation was there, and it was that which I had to build on.

Attending an evening worship service at Watson Temple, early fall of my Junior year following my surgery, I cried out to God and asked Him to forgive me, to save me, to come into my life and help me. I needed God's help every day. I was tired of the guilt, the shame, and just being angry.

I wanted my life back on the right path. Without a doubt, one

thing I knew that was always instilled in me was that Jesus

loves me. I didn't know why He would after some of the

things I had done, but He did, and I needed to feel His love

that night, every day. Jesus showed me, He filled me, and He

saved me.

Embracing the salvation I found, I tried to refocus on

finishing my degree and returning to my plan for my life. I

wanted to enjoy the college years that I had left. My

roommate decided to get her own place, so she would be in a

1 bedroom, and I would be in a 1 bedroom in the same

apartment complex upstairs. Of course, being on my own

would have its positives and negatives, but most of all, it was

a time for me to totally focus on what I needed to get back to

some level of normalcy and focus on graduating.

Trying not to focus on the pain and embarrassing things that

happened to me, I focused on accounting, collegiate ministry,

and joining organizations and clubs that would keep me busy.

I didn't want to be a victim; I just wanted to be normal. I didn't want to talk about the rape at all. Even though date rape was so prevalent on campus and was talked about all the time, I didn't ask for help. I just wanted to move on. Trying to complete that last year of school was difficult, especially in dealing with a challenging curriculum. By getting involved in business school organizations, collegiate ministry, and gospel choir, I met some great students who became some of my closest friends. I was also trying to maintain celibacy, carrying the hurt and distrust for men. As a result, I pushed away what some women would consider nice guy or good men.

I met men in the business school who wanted to date or start something more serious with me. Of course, my interaction was somewhat guarded. I tried to date and after nine months with one guy, he met my parents and I met his parents. He got involved in the church with me, yet the closer he got, the more I tried to find something wrong with him. The questions and conflict in my mind continued: *Why would*

he want me? If I was to tell him what really happened to me,
would he even still want me? I convinced myself that he was
crazy and broke up with him.

The next guy was a church boy with a beautiful voice;
he was a kind young man and a virgin. I couldn't even begin
to feel like I deserved to be with someone like him. He didn't
understand why I was afraid. I would hurt him and couldn't
explain or put the burden on him of trying to be that person
to help me love him the way he deserved. Being in a
relationship was not anything that I took lightly; the trust
issue I had was a big problem. I knew I would hurt him,
because I hurt the one before him badly, and I never told
either one of them the whole truth. All I knew was I still was
not in a place to accept or believe somebody would love me
the way either of them did. The low self-esteem, insecurities,
and guilt did not allow me to accept or recognize love.
Instead, I punished myself for what happened. I was not over
it and because of that, I did not allow myself to experience
being loved by someone else. Over the course of two years, I

turned down two marriage proposals and walked away from a half dozen relationships.

During my senior year, I began teaching, ministering, and began a bible study group on campus with my old roommate. Being with the other students and sharing God's word gave me life, Studying God's word together, and building spiritual connections with them helped me. Feeling God's love and experiencing it with others helped me begin to love myself again. I began consuming myself with not only finishing school but also being involved in collegiate ministry, choir, and bible studies whenever time allowed. Staying busy was a way of coping for me. As I grew in my relationship with God, I also realized I didn't want to be alone anymore. Not having anyone when my old roommate was in a steady relationship and all my friends had boyfriends and girlfriends; be alone was becoming something I no longer enjoyed. I had pushed so many guys away because I didn't feel I could love, but slowly God was opening my heart, as I shared his love through mentoring, teaching, and ministering in choir. I wanted that closeness, to love and be loved, and was ready to experience someone loving me again.

Fighting for Freedom

Finding comfort in a love for God's word and worshipping with friends at church and in choir rehearsals gave me life. I had a desire for more companionship, to meet a guy who shared the same passion for life, enjoyed serving others, and could love me just the way I was. Maybe this time, I would not run him away as I had done in the year past.

It was summer of 1996, my former roommate and friends I started FSU with, had just graduated and the summer was ending. Going into my last year of college, I met this man at Watson Temple. This guy was just different. He had a fire for God and a praise in his heart that would have him dancing up and down the aisles at church on any given Sunday. He was not part of the collegiate friends I shared; he was a transplant to Tallahassee being housed by a minister at the church. I assumed like most of us attending Watson Temple, that he was attending college somewhere in Tallahassee. We began to have conversations to get to know each other better. Immediately, I was attracted to his devotion to prayer and study of God's word. We just clicked, and our conversations were always intriguing. By attending the same church, we were at the same bible study, weekday service, and Sunday morning worship, so we were able to see each other every day.

Only when we began discussing his family did the conversation change; he would become silent or defensive. But I never questioned his story about his family life growing up or how he ended up in Tallahassee because he never gave me a reason not to trust him. If he said he would do something, he did it. If he said he was going to be somewhere, he normally was. We became like best friends, going everywhere together for the short months that we seriously dated. We shared everything from food to prayers every night. I was in love and it felt real and I felt no fear this time.

I finally had the chance to meet his mom and brother over the phone when we told them we were getting married, but I still had not had an opportunity to really know his family. He met my parents, and though they were happy for me, they really hoped I would wait to get married. We wanted to be married and we didn't want to wait any longer. I felt if we didn't, he would leave, and I would be alone again. We got married less than six months after meeting. So, I graduated with my Bachelors' degree in December of 1996 as a married woman.

I decided to accept my first job in Panama City, FL, a place I had never lived, almost hour and half away and had no family or friends near. My new husband and I drove to the city twice looking at places to live to start our new lives while enjoying the beautiful Panama City beaches. I remember the beautiful white soft sands and sounds of the ocean as if it was yesterday. Sitting on those sands together on a blanket enjoying each other's company was peaceful. Each time we went, I had so much joy being there. We would find a new place and though we didn't know a soul in the area, it was ours. We were excited to start new in our own place.

Less than four months after our relocation, things began to change. It was difficult for my husband to find good work full time because his education was not complete, which I was not aware of until that little problem came up. He explained to me his hostile relationship with his mother, which caused him to be put out in high school. He lived with relatives, friends and at some point, became homeless. While homeless he experimented with drugs and began smoking. Discussions with my husband about his lack of education and some of the addictions that he faced, caused him to get so defensive that I stopped talking about it. His anger and resentment were apparent to me and sometimes troubling. Trying to help him get a GED or find something that motivated him, only added to the frustration. He found part-time employment at a store near the apartment, which was convenient since we shared vehicle. At first, it didn't really bother me for him to drop me off at work or for me to drop him off, but on one lunch break, things began to unravel.

I smelled smoke on his clothes while doing the laundry and he got upset because I accused him of smoking cigarettes. That argument led into another argument when he began saying things to me about my appearance that I had not ever heard him say. I knew he was in a bad mood, tired of his convenience store job and always on the defensive about everything recently. But We mostly argued about church and religion; he tried to send me to hell on a regular for being Pentecostal instead of Apostolic. The Apostolic faith believes in God, the Pentecostal faith also believes in God. The difference is the Pentecostal faith teaches the Trinity; the father, the son, and the holy ghost. The Apostolic faith is Jesus only; no trinity. He would often tell me that my family did not believe as he believed and because of this I was going to burn in hell and so was all my family. If we did not repent in get baptized in "In Jesus Name" we were all going to hell. But, this argument about faith and religious beliefs was different; he began attacking my character, my appearance and I can remember him saying I was "ugly, stink, and homely looking and who would want" me! Not only had I never been talked to in that manner by another man before, but I was also hearing it from the very man I had just given my heart to and married less than 6 months prior.

On that day, during my lunch, while in this heated argument, I don't remember my words to him. I just remember having this urge to just get away from him while he was lashing out in anger, but whatever I said in response at that moment enraged him, so in a rage of anger he picked up my handful of keys and threw them at my face. He threw the keys so hard and so fast that they stuck in the wall next to my face, missing me by a few inches. I cannot tell you what I said, but my thought was *run*. I took off for the front door down the hall, but he grabbed me and would not let me go. He was so strong and in a rage; I feared for my life. I had nothing to fight with, but I tried with all my might to get out of the grips of his arms. I remember him saying, "You're not going nowhere. You're going to stay here with me. You're not going anywhere!" I kept telling him, "No, let me go, let me go!" He reacted by holding me tighter and tighter. Finally, as a last attempt to break free from his clutch on me, I took my nails and scratched so deeply into his hands that he had to let me go. I sprinted out of the apartment door, running and crying, but making it to the apartment office where I asked the receptionist to call the police. Crying, scared, and visibly shaken to the staff they called the police and asked me what happened. I didn't know what to think or to say, what just happened and why? When the police finally arrived, they talked to him first. He was cool, calm, and collected; the police officers saw his scratches before coming to take my story. They asked me what happened, had this ever happened before, and when they asked if I wanted to press charges for domestic violence assault and have a restraining order, I replied, "Yes." I was so conflicted about my answer though, I was pressing charges against my husband, the only real family I had in a place where I knew no one. Not knowing what to do and where to go, the process was confusing and hard. I was in a new city and not familiar with the laws and the process. All I had in Panama was the church I had just joined, co-workers, and the husband who just hurt me.

Alone, isolated, scared, and in total shock, all kinds of emotions, questions, and thoughts went through my head. *Did I just have my husband locked up? Was I overreacting like he told the cops? Maybe I shouldn't have made him so upset and kept asking him questions. What did I say to make him so mad? He thinks I am ugly, and I dress homely? Why would he say that I stunk? Oh my God, what did I just do?* Little did I know this incident was only the beginning of a cycle of him apologizing to get the injunction dropped to come back and begin to terrorize me weekly.

I moved for the second time after a few months. Believing him that things would be different, I let him back in the house. I remember coming home from work one day and finding all my high school memorabilia, including my senior book with all my awards, pictures of friends, prom souvenirs, athletic pins, and cheerleader ribbons, floating in a sink full of water in the kitchen. I screamed and cried over the sink non-stop, asking, *Why? Why would someone be so evil?* Precious items that could not be replaced from my high school memories were floating in a sink full of water ruined forever! *What would make someone do something so heartless and devious? What did I do to make him hurt me like this? Where is he?*

I went from sadness to rage. I was about to lose it; my mind was overwhelmed with anger. I knew whenever he did appear it was not going to be good. I began thinking what I can do to get him back, revenge was at the forefront of my mind. I was about to lose my mind. My Pastor and a few friends at church knew some of my struggle, but none of them knew I was at my breaking point that night. My family still did not know exactly the depth of the abuse that was going on in my marriage. I called my father crying. My heart was hurt, and my body was aching. I could hardly breathe as I attempted to explain what had been going on in my life. My dad advised me to contact my Pastor at the time. We connected that night, and she provided me not only comfort but safety by offering me a place to stay that night. I had exhausted my credit cards from staying in hotels in order to hide from my husband when he was in a bad mood or I didn't feel safe in my apartment. Greater Deliverance Church was my safe haven. I knew he would not hurt me there. I could worship, cry out to God, feel safe, and be with people who were concerned for me.

The day I will never forget was after he had run a revival in a small-town east of Panama City. Yes, a revival! My Pastor accompanied me to speak with my husband's Pastor. The entire time my husband's Pastor allowed him to continue to minister and preach at their church while committing domestic violence assault and battery. We had not attended the same church since my husband started being physically and verbally abusive. But on this night in 1998 I don't remember what the argument was about when he got physical and pushed me. I was angry and pushed back! I had to defend myself because I was sure he would try to kill me this time. We scuffled into the kitchen and over the sink, but I had nothing in my reach. No knife. No pot. Nothing! He had me wrapped up and would not let me go. His arms wrapped around me, and he pressed me against the counter I had to make him let me go! I opened my mouth and bit him on his chest and I kept my teeth clinched until he hollered and released me from what felt like a vice grip. I ran as fast as I could, but he caught me before I could get out of the front door.

Then, my husband threw me on the couch, grabbed the pillows on the couch, and began to smother my face with the pillows. I could barely breathe and felt like I was soon going to take my last breath. He pressed down harder, putting all his weight on me as I kicked and tried to get the pillows off my face. All I could think about was the fact that I couldn't breathe, and my husband was trying to kill me, and I had to get him off me now! I had to fight, so I squirmed enough on the couch until I was able to push him off me. Finally, he fell off and onto the glass table, breaking it. I ran out of the house, got to my car, and drove to the police station. I got to the station shaken, bruised, crying, and screaming in a rage while filing yet another police report.

I still cannot put together specific details of that night like date and time. But so many emotions were involved, and everything escalated so quickly. I was dealing with the trauma of my husband trying to suffocate me on my couch, the fear that they may arrest me for fighting back, and what I would do next. The police at the station took my report. My husband was already on probation for domestic violence assault. Again, the officer asked if I wanted to press charges for domestic violence battery and have a restraining order. Again, I said yes. However, this time, the injunction would be permanent, and his sentence would be six months of jail time.

You would think having this violent person out of the apartment would have brought me peace and I could begin putting my life back together again, but the turmoil and emotions were overwhelming. I felt consumed with the shame and embarrassment of taking my husband back yet again, believing him, after his mother told me not to. Even after the court performed mental evaluations, they still released him after the second time I had him arrested. His Pastor still stood by him while I looked like a woman who wanted to exaggerate the situation. I was broken. I was hurting. The physical bruises were slowly fading, but my heart and mind were scarred for life. I simply wanted the pain to stop and the movie of being nearly smothered on my couch that kept replaying in my head to be over.

With my husband locked up, I had time to spend with my church family, working and worshipping. Getting busy again teaching the bible and serving others at the church kept me busy. My Pastor, Sherlene McClary a wise woman I know was sent by God to help deliver me, allowed me to work at whatever I found to do. Working with the youth and mentoring teenage girls became a passion. Sharing life lessons with them, God's word, and showing them options for their lives gave me a new purpose. My Pastor was developing a plan to create a new community outreach program and buy a facility to house youth for afterschool. Being a part of that project kept me busy and gave me something to look forward to as I dealt with the pain and shame that had not felt so real since college.

The LOVE Group *Ladies of Virtue Endure,* was born. From it, young teenage girls learned basic life principles, self-worth, career options, and how to carry themselves as young women. Being around these young ladies and sharing life experiences as well as biblical principles helped bring me out of the darkness. I felt myself feeling alive again, having a glimpse of the joy I once knew back in college. I started domestic violence victims' counseling to begin healing and decided to get my life back on track again.

Though my story did not end in Panama City, my job and marriage did after my husband was released. I did not marry to get divorced, but I filed a divorce after 2 years and 8 days. I left Panama City and returned home. The shame and hurt of returning home with no job and divorced were the most difficult things I had to do. Yet, I knew it was the only way for a new beginning and fresh start. I was returning to family and friends who had no idea the ordeal and life events that I had lived through the last few years. I immediately got busy trying to find employment, not just 1 job but 2. I had to save up some money, while paying off marital debt, and saving up for my own place.

Connecting with old friends and people with like minds was the key to getting back to a place of stability quickly. I received a referral for a job by my long-time friend who eventually became my Pastor and mentor, Elder John Christian. Though I had mentored troubled teens and at-risk youth in Panama City, I had never been a social worker. But I accepted a job as a Foster Care Worker, working with youth who had been removed from their families due to abuse and neglect. Some of these children had been through such traumatic experiences that they suffered from depression and other psychotic disorders.

Meeting these children and reading their files made

my situation seem less traumatic while bringing back memories I had buried deep down. I met young people who had suffered sexual assault or abuse from other people in their household. I learned what molestation really was and realized I had been molested by a relative growing up. I was required to take sensitivity training and protective services training and began learning the magnitude of sexual abuse and domestic violence in families as well as how these children were exposed and damaged emotionally from these tragic events. I learned the actions taken by their parents or adults in their homes that could cause permanent emotional and psychological damage to these children if not addressed. Learning all the warning signs and resources to help these young people and their families were not only helping them get to healing but helping me as well. I worked full-time as a Social Worker, part-time as an Assistant Manager at a shoe store, and part-time as a tax preparer. I was busy trying to get my life back and learning myself all over again.

When I was not working one of my three jobs, I was

helping my mentor with a community outreach program called Men of Distinction. Men of Distinction provided after school alternatives for at risk teens. The community outreach program had counselors that worked with the teens to teach against tobacco use and drugs. A choir was formed, and the numbers of youth began to grow. Most of the at-risk youth that the organization served was teenage girls. Getting involved with them and helping organize the same format for the teenage girls I had in Panama City was nothing I had to think about too long. The DOVE group *Daughters of Virtue Endure,* was started, and so I began again. I had an opportunity to share with these ladies more life experiences, but this time, I knew more resources and connections to help them make better choices. With the help of my mentor and soon to be Pastor, along with one of my best friends, we encouraged and empowered these young ladies to follow their dreams, endure temptations, and be all that God would have them to be. Working with this group of young women and sharing God's word with them along with my co-

counselor gave me purpose again.

Months had passed, and the divorce was final, so I started dating, but not really for the right reasons. I was broken and didn't really trust men and definitely not a man in the church. I returned to Leesburg angry, disappointed, and hurt. Not only was I divorced, but I also found out before I left Panama City that I was infertile. I had polycystic ovarian syndrome. According to my specialist, the only way I could conceive was with help from drugs or surgery. It was one more disappointment that felt like a life sentence because of my past. Yet, I served the young ladies who were being promiscuous and not even trying to get pregnant but were having babies before they could even graduate from high school. This reality caused me more pain, and I didn't know how to get past it. But I knew I couldn't dwell on it. I was no longer married, and dating was really not something I did well, so having a baby was not a concern, because I was not getting married anytime soon.

Finally FREE

Three years later, my Pastor started Christian Worship Center, a church in the same building our community outreach program had begun in some years prior. It was an exciting time because I also got married to my new husband in July of 2001. We had been dating during the time I was serving as a mentor with the DOVE group. He was not a minister, not affiliated with the outreach program, but a hardworking man, with a great smile that enjoyed my companionship as much as I enjoyed his company over the last couple of years. There was no spectacular proposal or anything we just decided we loved each other, and we were getting married. My Pastor did the honors of doing marriage counseling and marrying us.

Our newly organized church Christian Worship Center was hosting our first Women's Conference, and my Pastors asked me to share my testimony of date rape in college. I thought I would be afraid, but I was not. I thought I was going to be embarrassed, but by that point, I was not. I saw my mom, fellow church members, and conference attendees sitting there as I began to tell the details of my college tragedy of date rape. I shed some tears, but they were no longer tears of sadness; they were tears of relief. My mom visibly was hurt that I had been silent so long. Holding all that frustration and anger in of what happened to me for all those years but, I almost felt like I could breathe again because the secret was out finally. It was a weight that I carried that was keeping me from moving forward.

My new husband at the time did not have all the details of my tragic past either, but what we soon found out after the conference was my miracle happened: I was pregnant! God had given me my miracle. I had travelled to fertility specialist and they couldn't help me get pregnant, but God took all my messes and gave me a message through the journey of infertility. Because I was willing and obedient and shared my struggle, God gave me the desires of my heart. He gave me a new husband and a baby boy. Almost seven years later, he gave me another baby boy. Without me asking for another miracle, it happened.

Each time tragedies in my life arrived, God used His grace and mercy to bring me out of the pit I was slowly sinking into daily. The hurt, anger, disappointment, tragedies, and low self-esteem felt like it would bury me so far that I would try and isolate myself from everyone. Yet, it was true, God's love and forgiveness and kindness towards me, saved me.

Each time I found myself sinking, something inside reminded me of God's love again and his mercy towards me. I began surrounding myself with the things of God like serving others, whether it be pouring into another young person and sharing my struggles and pain or volunteering my time; my attitude and mindset changed. I no longer focused on me but on serving God's people, regardless of what I was dealing with mentally or emotionally. God took care of me and gave me what to say and how to say it to minister to His young people. He gave me a gift to share with others to help empower them and bring them in, to show them that love that God showed me when I needed it, and God would do the rest. When I was at my lowest point in Panama City, reliving the pain and embarrassment of rape, being battered by someone who was supposed to be a minister of God, ending a failed marriage, and the last dagger, losing my job, I remember driving to Panama City Beach one evening, parking the car at the ocean, and crying. I don't remember how long I sat at that ocean sobbing, feeling like I let myself down, my family down, but once I was done, the tears drying off my cheeks as the ocean breeze blew gently across my face. I sat and listened to the ocean, I felt a sense of peace and serenity. I made a promise to myself that I would not allow myself to live in a state of unhappiness again. I thanked God for sparing my life but promised myself that whatever situation I found myself in, I would not wake up living in anger, fear, and unhappiness another day. Life was not to be taken for granted; I must commit to live.

After about 10 years of marriage, thinks began to

unravel and be tested. The hurt that was never discussed in my past and the pain and grief that my husband had in his life that had never been addressed became toxic to our marriage. I took a new job in Tampa, FL and this would be our new beginning to try and make things better between us again. The move away brought additional challenges being away from family support and my church family and friends. Learning to depend on each other as husband and wife, to seek out resources to help with the kids, and the stress of a new job in a big City became overwhelming fast. My parents were my rock and always helped me with my 2 boys. My church family were my support and always had my back and my Pastor I could go to for advice about anything and now I had no one to turn to, but to trust God.

On December 8, 2013 I suffered a pulmonary embolism. I was hospitalized for 3 days and as I lay there that first night in the emergency room, I kept playing in my mind what the ER Physician said to me. He said, "mam had you fallen asleep, the clots would have collapsed your lung, and you just would not have wakened." I could have died! I would have died in my sleep worn out, tired, and unhappy. I was told that I would be out of work at least 3 months by the physicians and may or may not be able to return full time. The hospital physicians suggested I apply for permanent disability and possibly not return to work at all. But I could not accept that. It just didn't feel right in my mind and in my spirit. God let me live and all I could do was be grateful for his grace and mercy, again! *"I shall live and not die"* was all I kept feeling in my spirit. God made me whole after I turned to Him again after that blood clot that traveled through my heart and broke into pieces in my lungs, almost taking my life. I went from laying in a hospital for those 3 days, to laying at home on a couch for weeks, going back and forth to blood labs and doctors, with nothing but time to think about everything bad that happened in my life prior to that day: the fatigue of the illness, the negative emotions, a marriage in turmoil, and a state of anxiety were all overwhelming me. Still, God sent messages from family and friends to encourage me by phone and text. He reminded me of His grace and mercy, "I shall live and not die."

What could have killed me with the clots in my blood ended up saving me from self-destruction. My marriage was not working, and I was unhappy, but I had time to self-reflect on my part in the demise of the union. I was a broken woman when I got married the second time and remained a broken woman who was wounded and needed to be made whole. I felt like the woman with the issue of blood described in the New Testament who needed God to not only fix my blood in the physical by removing the clots trying to kill me, but also to fix me in the spirit from the demons of my past who were keeping me from moving forward emotionally. I wanted to be made whole.

I wanted not just happiness; I wanted my joy back. I wanted the joy I felt when I knew the peace of God was with me. A joy that could not be shaken by one bad memory, but a joy that made me immediately thank God and smile because I could have been dead. I sought God in daily prayer and communion to heal me, deliver me, and make me whole. However, I didn't stop there; I decided to seek professional counseling, to help me deal with my hurts of the past, the demise of my current marriage, and the post trauma of the pulmonary embolism. Regular therapy sessions and my daily communion with God, changed everything. My mind, body, and soul felt free again.

Nearly 20 years to the date of that night, I am living and truly living in freedom. It has been a process. The journey has not been easy, but God knows it has been worth it. I have gained valuable life lessons that could have only been learned through some hard tests. I am a work in process, but I am not what happened to me. One hundred miles away from my hometown, two miracle children, two divorces, and one life-threatening pulmonary embolism later, I can say that I am a free mind, body, and soul.

To get to Free, I had to learn to face my truth as well as acknowledge the truth about who I really am in God. For me to acknowledge who I am in God, I had to see and love myself the way God does, which required some work. The work began with forgiving the people who had hurt me in the past and forgiving myself for the decisions that I made as a teenager, as a young adult, and the secrets that I kept from my friends and family. I had to forgive the men that hurt me, even though they never apologized; this type of forgiveness was much harder than I thought. Forgiving a person who claimed to love God was even harder, but it became easier once I realized that what he did could not stop me and did not stop me. The anger and embarrassment were no longer present. God made me stronger. In fact, I had grown in wisdom because of it.

God began renewing my mind. I began thinking differently about my life and what I wanted to do, and the purpose God had for me. God gave me the strength and stamina to work through my healing process emotionally and physically. My outlook on life was different; my heart desired to live and laugh daily. I wanted my joy back. Renewing my mind with positive thoughts and positive people in a positive environment meant losing my marriage and finding new employment. I made a conscious decision to do that. It was not easy or popular, but I was willing to do whatever I had to get to peace.

Through the process of going to counseling, taking divorce and parenting classes, and learning about the cycles of domestic violence and sexual violence in families, I became even more motivated to do something. Through me, God birthed a non-profit dedicated to empowering people to overcome the effects of sexual violence and domestic violence in their lives. This organization would provide solutions through resources that encourage a lifestyle of victory over violence one day at a time. Established in October 2017, Victory Over Violence, of FL Inc., is a mission God gave me, and He has made provisions for me to change lives in my community and all over the country with a message of freedom, courage, and victory.

Getting to FREE

To be Free means you are not physically restrained; nothing is impeding you; you are no longer under the power or control of another. You have been released from captivity, confinement, or slavery.

Freedom is gained through a four – step process:

o **Forgiving of Others and Yourself**

First, we must forgive others, releasing ourselves from the bondage that unforgiveness puts on our hearts and mind. Forgiveness can be difficult especially when the perpetrator of sexual and domestic abuse often has never apologized. To be truly free, we must let it go!

A second part to forgiveness is forgiving ourselves. Realizing it's not your fault regardless of how the abuse, assault, or traumatic circumstances happened; it's NOT your fault. The guilt and shame may have caused you to feel less than, never good enough, never pretty/handsome enough but you are not what happened to you. You are fearfully and wonderfully made in the image of God, who made you for His service and to worship Him through your life. Your pain had a purpose. So, you must forgive you!

_____

_____

_____

_____

_____

_____

_____

o **Renewing of Your Mind**

Renewing of your mind follows forgiving yourself because you must change the way you see yourself. The negative thoughts that enter your mind automatically due to the toxicity that you may have been living in for so long must become positive messages and affirmations about who you really are in Christ. You are no longer afraid; you are courageous. You are no longer bound; you are free in mind, body, and soul. You are not a victim; you are a survivor. You are victorious, you are more than a conqueror, and you can do all things through Christ who will give you strength.

_____

_____

_____

_____

_____

_____

○ **Educating Yourself**

Education about the trauma that affected your life and the ways it affected/affects your family, specifically children and others who witnessed the abuse or assault, is powerful. Becoming aware and addressing the issues with proper counseling or therapy is critical in the healing process. Mental health is important in healing the mind, body, and soul. It helps to build healthy relationships moving forward and strengthen the family.

Prayer is great when dealing with trauma and during the healing process. Prayer is a daily necessity, but God also gives gifts; He has given people wisdom to share with others to help them heal emotionally; however, we must be willing to access those resources and get the assistance to live healthy after the pain.

o **Empowering Others**

Empower means to give the authority to do something; to make someone stronger and more confident, specifically in controlling their life and claiming their rights. You can do that when you have truly been set free. Once you have forgiven others and yourself, are living in peace in a renewed state of mind, have educated yourself on the effects of the trauma, have addressed the trauma head on and faced it, you can share the journey with others. Speaking up and standing up to any type of abuse or assault is not easy but necessary to save the next life. It's important because many people live in pain daily; they choose to hide secrets of their past, not wanting to say anything due to the guilt, shame, and ridicule that accompanies them. You empower these hurting people every time you tell your story. Tell of your struggles and how you have overcome them as we learned growing up in the church; share your testimony, for you will set someone Free!

Victory Over Violence of FL, Inc. was established on October 16, 2017, by Lorrie A. Simmons due to an overwhelming need to bring awareness of the effects of domestic violence and sexual violence in families within her community. Lorrie has been ministering and mentoring for over 22 years. A survivor and overcomer of sexual violence and domestic violence, Lorrie's vision is to empower people with education and connect victims to resources, so they can walk in victory over violence one day at a time.

Principles to live by for Victory Over Violence

I am no longer afraid; I am courageous   Psalm 31:14-24

I am no longer bound; I am free   Job 11:15-18

I am no longer a victim; I am victorious   Psalm 118:14-21

For more information about the non-profit and its efforts in the community or to offer support, visit:

www.victoryoverviolencefl.com

Resources

Florida Coalition Against Domestic Violence

www.fcadv.org

National Coalition Against Domestic Violence

www.ncadv.org

The Haven of Lake & Sumter Counties

www.havenlakesumter.org

HOPE Family Services www.hopefamilyservices.org

The Spring of Tampa Bay www.thespring.org

Still Standing Alliance https://thestillstandingalliance.org

About the Author

Lorrie Brinson Simmons is an advocate for bringing awareness of the prevalence and effects of domestic violence and sexual violence in families across various communities. Due to her experiences of sexual violence through date rape, domestic violence at the hands of her first husband, and old wounds brought into a second marriage, Lorrie is able to provide a sympathetic view and share how to become a survivor, rather than identify as a victim of domestic and sexual violence.

Lorrie shares how her faith in God allowed her to continue to move forward despite the damaging physical and mental effects of domestic and sexual violence. She was able to earn a Master's Degree in Accounting, raise two boys, and continue to minister in and out of the church…and *no,* it was not easy, but possible.

Lorrie's experiences, love for people, and desire for all to be *FREE* prompted her to start a non-profit organization, Victory Over Violence of FL, Inc., to provide a place of connection for those personally dealing with domestic and sexual violence and those who know someone in domestic and sexual violence situations.

Free is Lorrie's life story that shares the rollercoaster emotions that domestic and sexual violence bring, such as depression, guilt, lack of forgiveness, anger, rage, shame, embarrassment and hopelessness. *Free* offers spiritual advice and practical guidelines through a four-step process for overcoming these emotions as well as the "I Am" principles to live by. Lorrie wants all to know that your pain can produce purpose, and you can overcome and be *Free*: *Free* from it all!

Made in the USA
Columbia, SC
24 May 2021